# Contents

## Me and my class

- 2. About me
- 4. What am I good at?
- 5. My class
- 6. Where do we come from?
- 8. Our classroom
- 9. Our Essential Agreements

## The learner profile

- 10. Inquirer
- 12. Knowledgeable
- 14. Thinker
- 16. Communicator
- 18. Principled
- 20. Open-minded
- 22. Caring
- 24. Risk-taker
- 26. Balanced
- 28. Reflective
- 30. Reflecting on my learner profile

## Social skills

- 32. Showing our feelings
- 33. Working through worries
- 34. Other people's feelings
- 35. Being a good friend

## Self-management skills

- 36. Favourite places in my classroom
- 37. Ways to calm down
- 38. What kind of learner am I?
- 39. The way I learn
- 40. My goal

## Communication skills

- 42. Pictures tell a story
- 44. Being a good listener and speaker
- 46. Practising my speaking skills
- 47. Hiding treasure

## Thinking skills

- 48. Critical thinking
- 50. Creative thinking
- 53. Reflecting on my day

## Research skills

- 54. Using my senses
- 55. Questions or facts?
- 56. Finding out more
- 57. Thinking about questions

## Class projects and reflection

- 58. Class projects
- 63. Reflecting on my year
- 64. How have I changed this year?

 About me

This is what I look like …

Words to describe me … Place  here:

Things I like …

Things I don't like …

# What am I good at?

I'm good at …

I'm learning how to …

💭 What can you do to get better at these?

4

 **My class**

Draw your classmates inside the house.

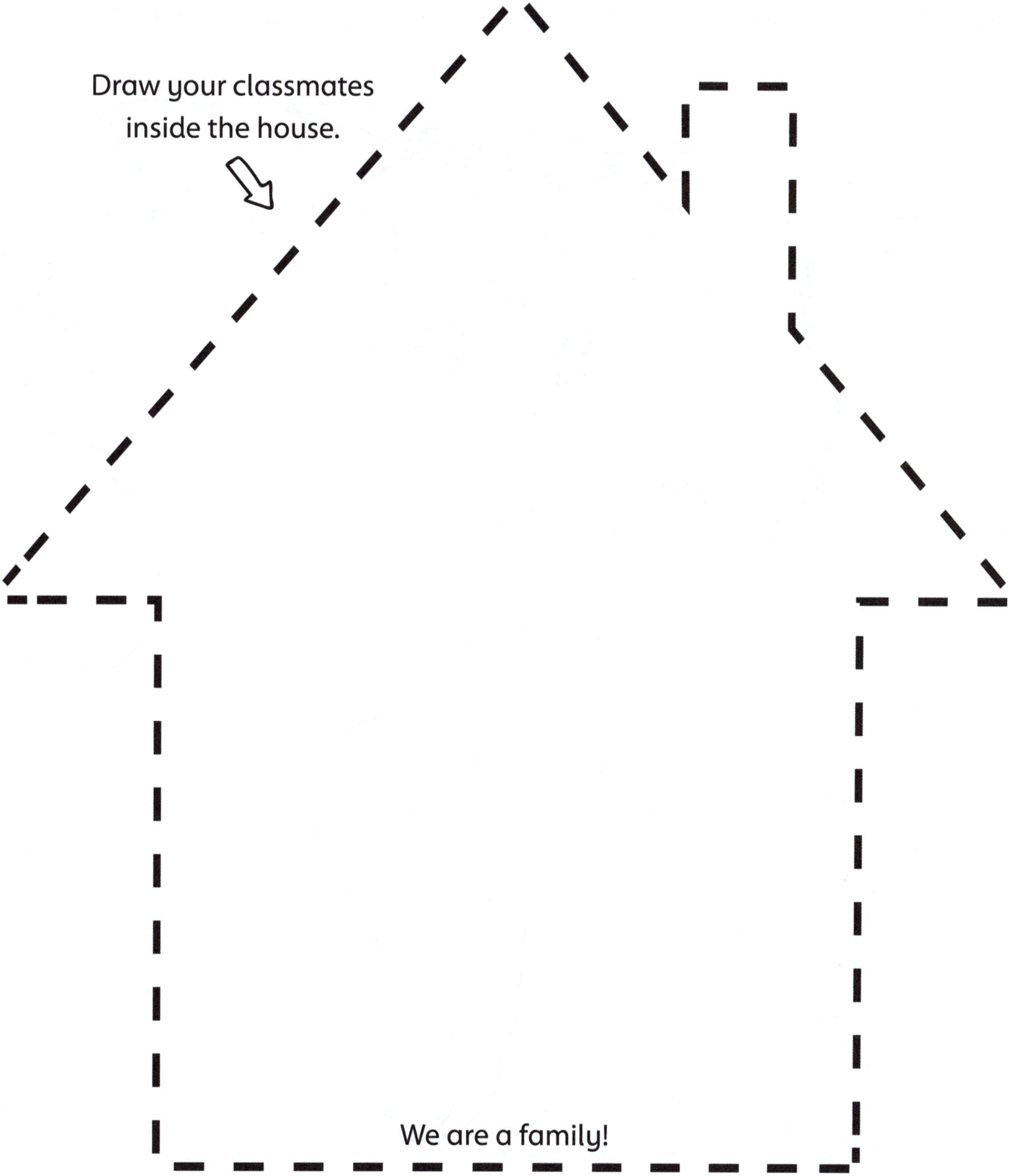

We are a family!

 # Where do we come from?

Add stick figures to the map to show where your classmates come from.

# Our classroom

Think about your school.
Add your ideas.

*What do I enjoy about school?*

*How can I help others at school?*

💬 What is important in a classroom?

A good classroom is …    safe

 # Our Essential Agreements

Draw the agreements that are most important to you.

 Where are the essential agreements shown in your classroom?

# Inquirer

Our learner profiles can help us to become better people and learners.

Here are some ways you can be an **inquirer**:

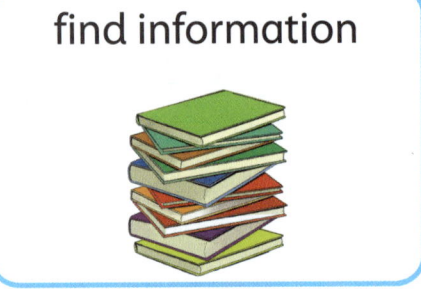

Think about how you are an **inquirer**.

**Draw and write about yourself being an inquirer.**

I am an inquirer when I ...

# Knowledgeable

Here are some things you can be **knowledgeable** about:

Think about how you are **knowledgeable**.

I know a lot about animals.

Draw and write about yourself being **knowledgeable**.

I am knowledgeable when I …

# Thinker

Here are some ways you can be a **thinker**:

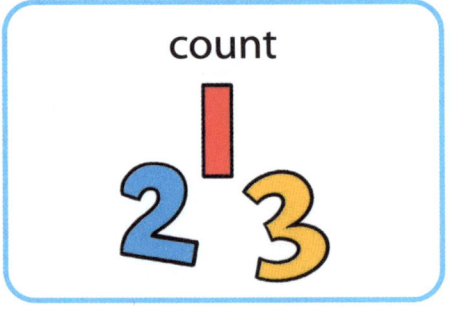

What makes you a **thinker**?

Draw and write about yourself being a **thinker**.

I am a thinker when I ...

# Communicator

Here are some ways you can be a **communicator**:

Think about how you are a **communicator**.

Draw and write about yourself being a **communicator**.

I am a communicator when I …

# Principled

Here are some ways you can be **principled**:

 be honest

 be kind

 share

 be thoughtful

 be friendly

Think about how you are **principled**.

I do what is right.

Draw and write about yourself being **principled**.

I am principled when I ...

# Open-minded

Here are some ways you can be **open-minded**:

explore

embrace differences

think about feelings

share

learn

Think about how you are **open-minded**.

I listen to others' ideas.

Draw and write about yourself being **open-minded**.

I am open-minded when I ...

# Caring

Here are some ways you can be **caring**:

help

be kind

look after friends

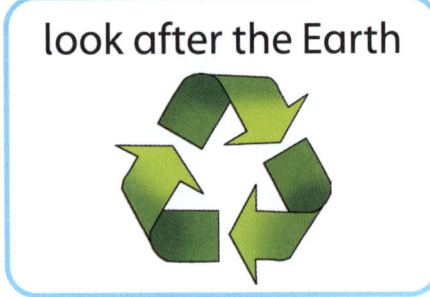
look after the Earth

think about feelings

Think about how you are **caring**.

I am kind.

Draw and write about yourself being **caring**.

I am caring when I …

# Risk-taker

Here are some ways you can be a **risk-taker**:

| explore | make mistakes | be brave |
|---|---|---|
|  |  |  |

| face fears | try new things |
|---|---|
|  |  |

Think about how you are a **risk-taker**.  *I try new things.*

24

Draw and write about yourself being a **risk-taker**.

I am a risk-taker when I ...

# Balanced

Here are some ways you can be **balanced**:

be healthy

have fun

learn

try new things

see new places

Think about how you are **balanced**.

I take care of myself.

Draw and write about yourself being **balanced.**

I am balanced when I ...

# Reflective

Here are some ways you can be **reflective**:

Think about how you are **reflective**.

I think about how to be better.

Draw and write about yourself being **reflective**.

I am reflective when I …

# Reflecting on my learner profile

Think about your learner profile.

What are you good at?

Do you need help with any of the learner profile attributes?

For example:

Draw or write your own attributes in the table.

| 🙂 I am good at these learner profile attributes | 😐 I need help with these learner profile attributes |
|---|---|
|  |  |

💬 Share your ideas with a partner. What do you notice?

# Showing our feelings

Our faces can show how we feel. If we notice our feelings, we can help ourselves and others.

Draw the feeling on each face.

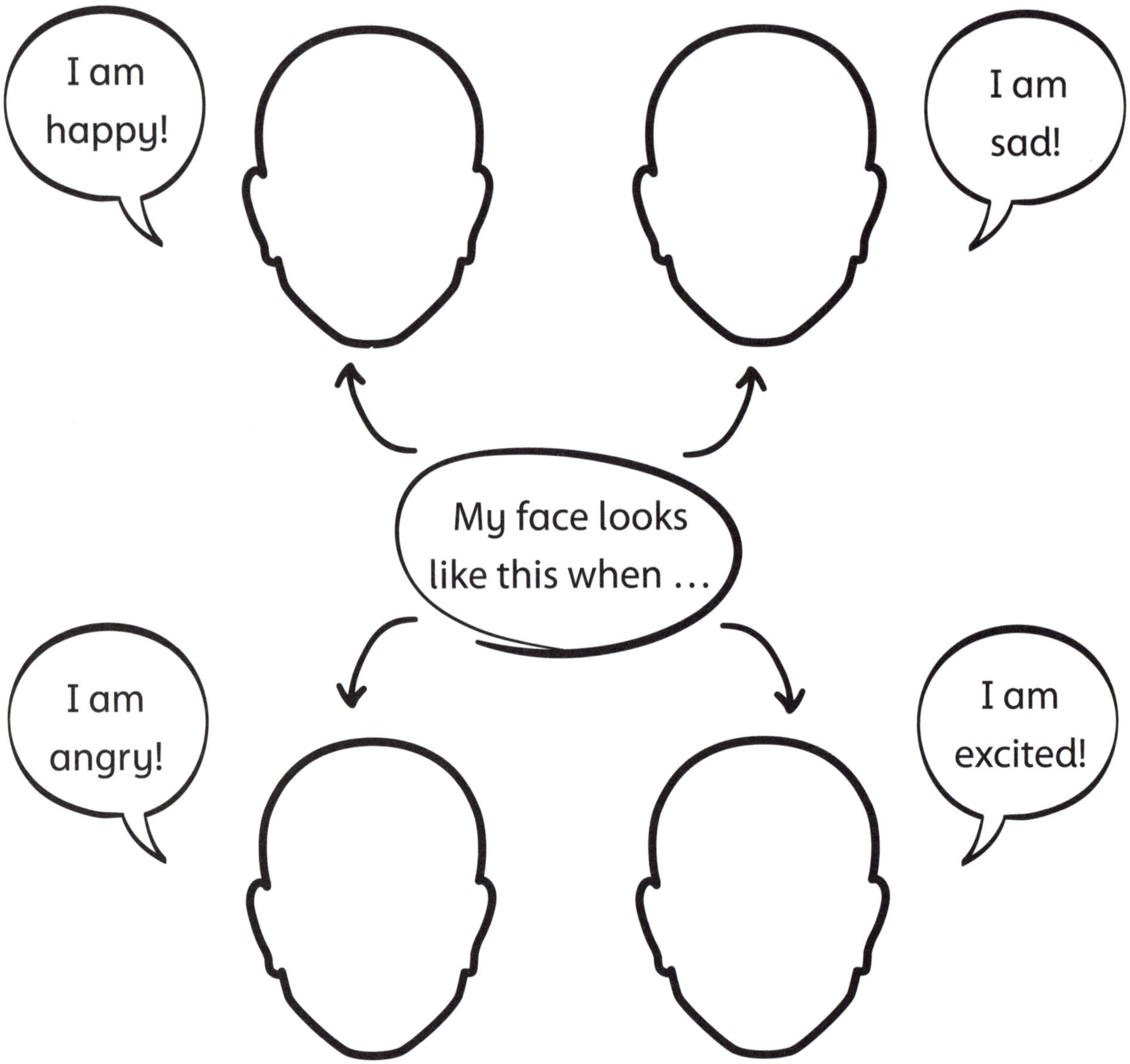

I am happy!

I am sad!

My face looks like this when …

I am angry!

I am excited!

💬 Talk to a partner about what makes you feel these emotions.

Complete this sentence: "When I feel ..............................................,

I want to .............................................................................................................."

# Working through worries

Different things can make you feel worried. Knowing what they are and talking about them can make you feel better.

What things make you feel worried? Write or draw them.

Share your worries with a friend. What do you notice? Are there some worries that are the same?

# Other people's feelings

How do you know when someone is feeling upset?

They might look like this …

Why might this boy be crying?

💬 Talk to a partner about what makes people upset.

💭 How can you be **caring** and help a friend if you see them looking sad?

# Being a good friend

A friend is a person you like and enjoy spending time with. Good friends help each other.

Think about your friends and how you would describe them.
Draw your friends below.

What words would you use to describe them?

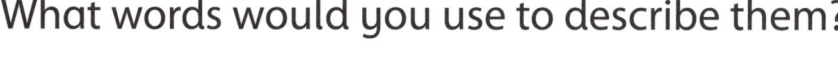

Are you a good friend? How can you be an even better friend?

# Favourite places in my classroom

We all have favourite places in our classroom. Be **open-minded** to exploring new areas.

My favourite places to play:

Pick a new place in the classroom where you might like to explore:

💬 Compare your favourite places with a partner's.
Talk about your favourite and least favourite places in the classroom.
Why do you feel that way?

# Ways to calm down

When you are feeling upset or worried, there are many ways to calm down.

A deep breath　　　　　Yoga　　　　　Music

Draw or write some things that help you feel calm.

 Share with a partner to see how they calm down.
As a class, think about how these ideas can be used in the classroom.

# What kind of learner am I?

**Which animal best describes you as a learner?**

"I have lots of energy."

"I like to take risks."

"I sort out problems."

"I learn quickly."

"I care for others."

"I know a lot of facts."

"I like to take my time."

Compare your ideas with others in your class.

Which animal do you want to be more like?

# The way I learn

How do you learn best? By yourself, with a partner or in a bigger group?

☐ ☐ ☐

Ask your classmates what they prefer. Add tally lines to the boxes.
One line means one person.

I learn best by myself:

I learn best with a partner:

I learn best in a group:

 What do you notice?

 Do your class essential agreements need to change?

39

# My goal

Be a **thinker**. Choose a skill you would like to improve.
For example, you might want to get better at …

My goal is ..................................................................................................

....................................................................................................................

....................................................................................................................

....................................................................................................................

Circle the people who will help you with your goal.

 Me!

 My family

 My friends

 My teacher

 How will you reach your goal?

Draw yourself reaching your goal!

When did you reach your goal?

 # Pictures tell a story

What is happening in the cartoon?

 Tell the story to a partner.

 Act out the story to your class.

Make your own cartoon. — Add speech bubbles if your characters talk.

 How else do we communicate our ideas and feelings?

 Play a game of 'charades' with a partner. Pretend to do an action. Can they tell what you're doing?

# Being a good listener and speaker

Practise being a good listener and speaker by playing this game.

1. Sit back-to-back with a partner.

2. Make something, but don't let your partner see. Then clearly tell them how to make it.

3. Swap. Then look at what each other has made!

Here are some ideas of things you could make …

I made this …

My partner made this …

💭 Did you enjoy the game? Were you a better speaker or listener? What did you find easy or hard?

# Practising my speaking skills

Bring your favourite toy to school to show your class.

Think about what to tell the class about your toy. Note your ideas.

- Where did you get it from?
- How does it work?
- Why is it special?
- Anything else?

Now it's your turn to talk. Remember …

☐ Speak loudly.

☐ Look at people.

☐ ............................................................................

☐ ............................................................................

💭 How did you feel after? Why?

💬 Ask your classmates how you could improve.

## Hiding treasure

**1** Think of a good place in the classroom to hide treasure.

**2** Draw a map of the classroom. Include tables, chairs and your hiding spot.

**3** Write instructions for how to get from the door to your treasure.

Go straight ⇧
Turn left ⇦
Turn right ⇨

Tell your instructions to a partner.
Can they work out where your treasure is?

# Critical thinking

Being a critical **thinker** means you think carefully and ask questions.

Do you think these pictures are real or fake?

Discuss your ideas with a partner. Make notes next to the pictures.

Draw your own fake picture.

Show your partner.

Can they spot what is fake about it?

48

Which one of these pictures is the odd one out?
Discuss your ideas with a partner. There is no right or wrong answer, but it is important to explain your reasons.

 How easy did you find this activity?
Colour the face that shows how you felt.

 # Creative thinking

How could these objects be connected? Draw lines to join the pictures.

 Share your ideas with a partner. What do you notice?

Let's be creative **thinkers**!

How could these everyday objects be used in different ways?

Share your ideas with a partner. What do you notice?

What other objects could you use in different ways?

 # Creative thinking

Being a creative **thinker** can help you come up with many answers to a problem.

Look at the pictures. What is the same? What is different?

 How might you sort or organize these pictures?

# Reflecting on my day

Think about what happened in your day. How did you feel?
What might you do differently tomorrow?

**My day**

I am feeling …

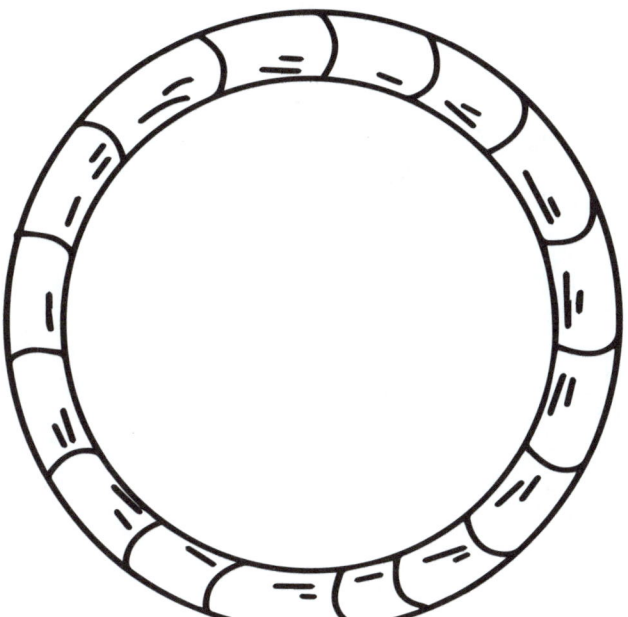

Today I learned …

I smiled when …

Tomorrow I will try to …

# Using my senses

Senses help us to understand the world around us.

Draw lines from the five senses to the body.

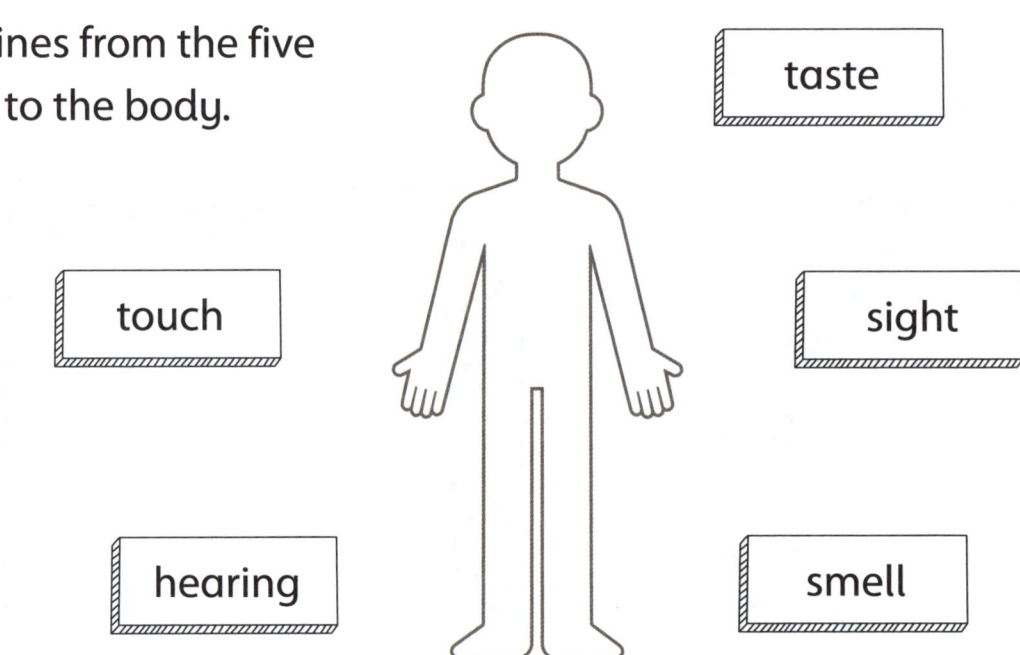

Who loves POPCORN?

Use your senses to think about this yummy snack. What does it look, smell, taste, sound and feel like?

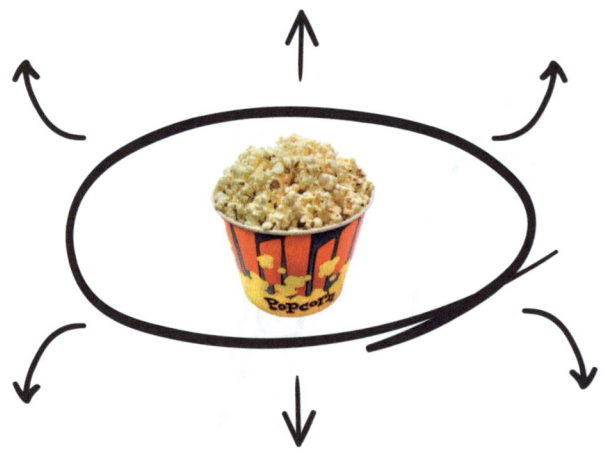

# Questions or facts?

Being an **inquirer** means you ask questions.
Being **knowledgeable** means you know facts.
What is the difference between a question and a fact?

Draw lines to show which of these sentences are questions, and which are facts.

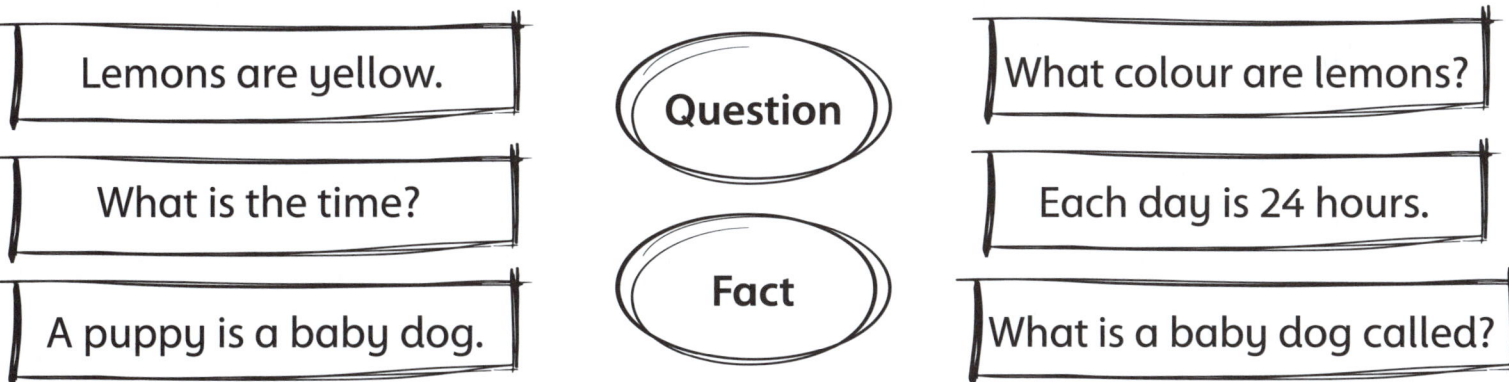

Write your own question and fact.

55

# Finding out more

 Write **three** words that you think of when you look at this picture.

> Use **3–2–1** to help you become a thinker.

 Write **two** ideas you have after looking at the picture.

I think ..............................................................................

..............................................................................

..............................................................................

 Write **one** question you have about this picture.

I wonder ..............................................................................

..............................................................................

Where can you find the answer to your question?

# Thinking about questions

Think about something you like. It could be an animal, a sport, a place or something else!

What questions do you have about it?

Why do flowers only grow in spring and summer?

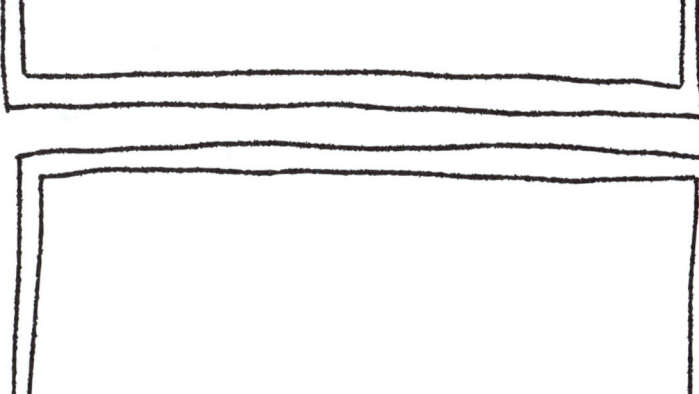

 As a class, create a 'Wonder Wall' and add your best questions.

 How might you find answers to all your amazing questions?

# Class project: Rubbish

Rubbish that we throw away can harm the Earth.

What can we do with our rubbish?
Think of ideas with a partner and share with the class.
Write or draw your ideas to create your own mind map.

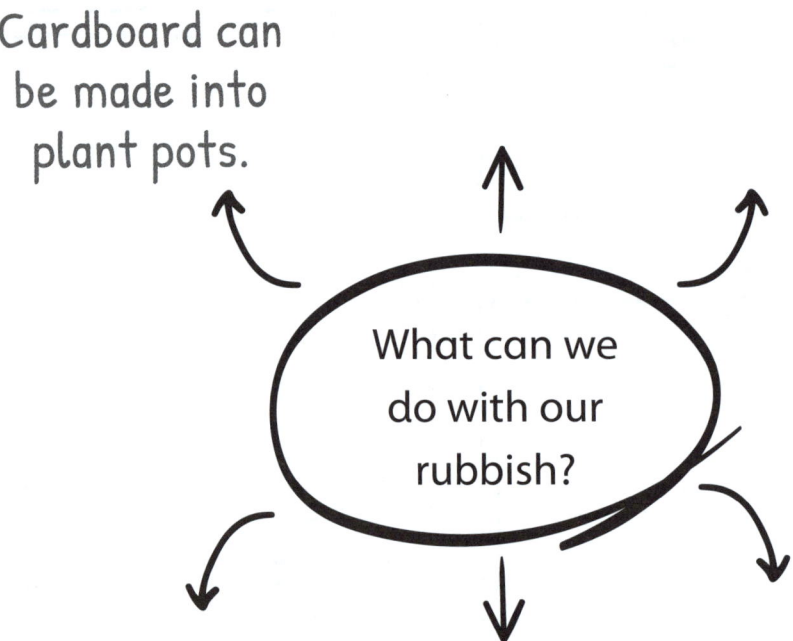

# Class project: Recycling

Recycling is a way of turning things into something new.

Show your **knowledge.** Draw these items in the correct recycling bins.

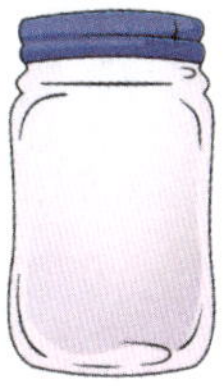

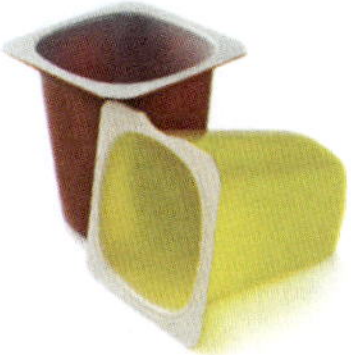

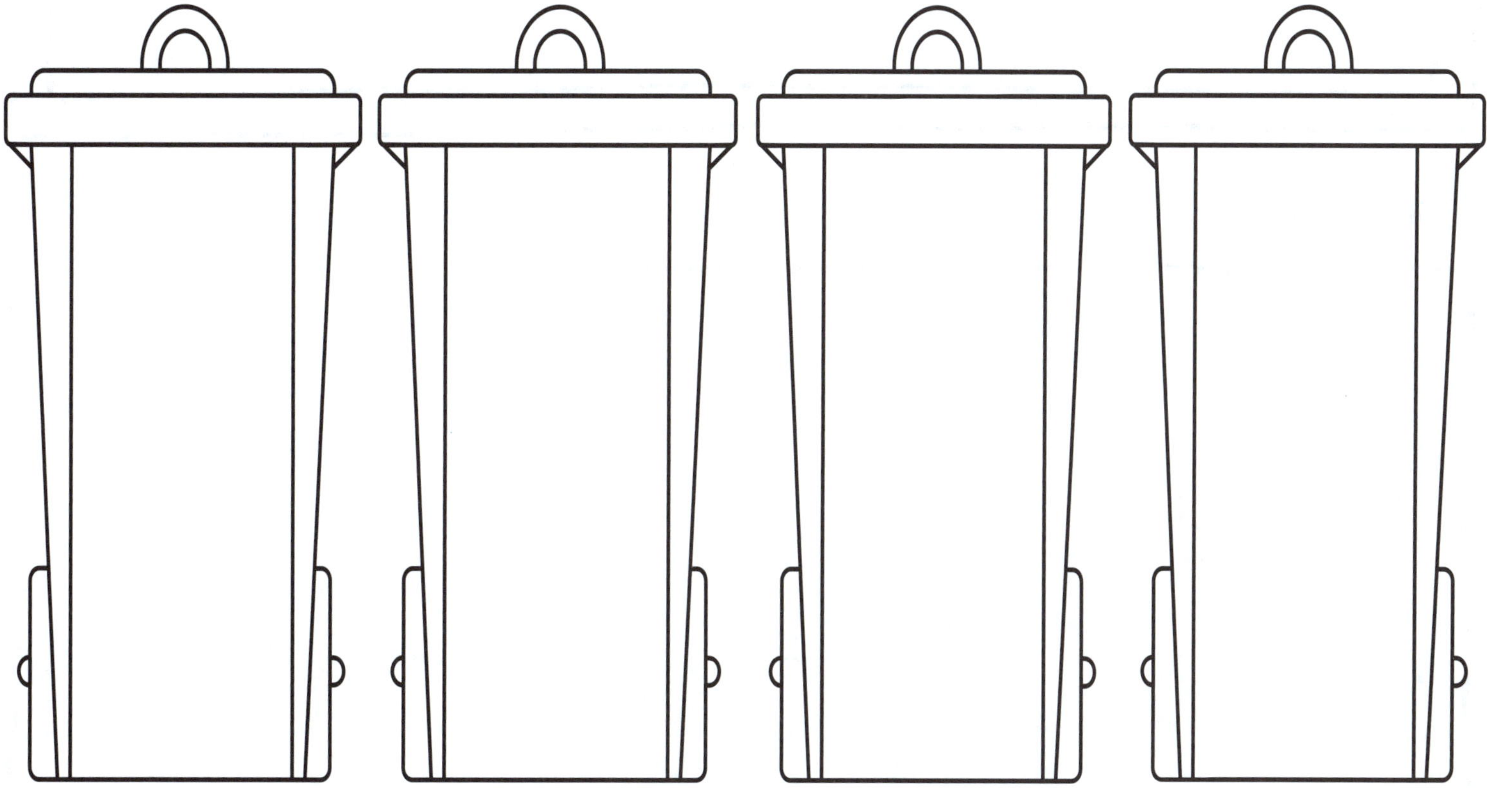

**Glass**  **Plastic**  **Food**  **Paper**

Bring in things from home that can be recycled.
Can you find a way to sort them together?

# Class project: Make something new

Have a look through the things that were brought in.
Think about what you could make.

I will make a …

I will need …

Talk about how you will make your new thing.
What are the steps?

# Class project: Personal reflection

I made this …

People who helped me …

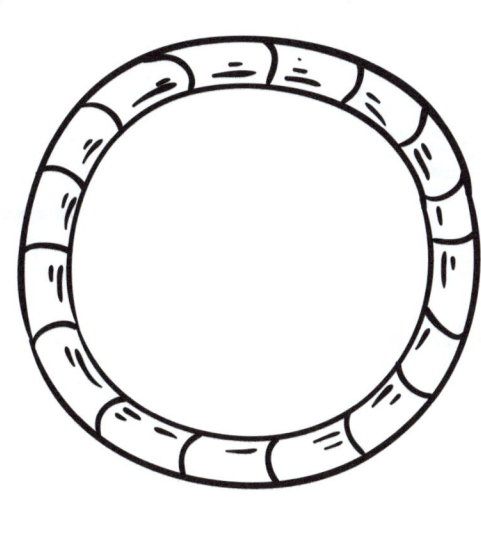

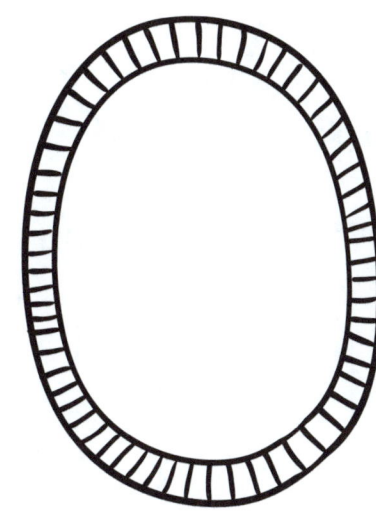

Reflect on what you made.

I really liked the way I …

I am most proud of …

Next time, I need to …

I wish I had …

# Class project: Taking action

How did this project make you feel?

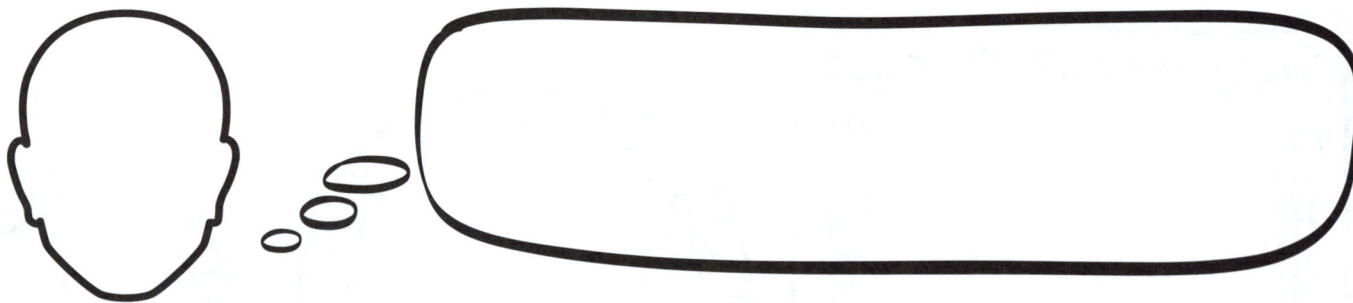

What else can you do to help our planet?

💬 Discuss your ideas with a partner.

# Reflecting on my year

Something I learned …

Something I am proud of …

The learner profile attribute that I used the most was …

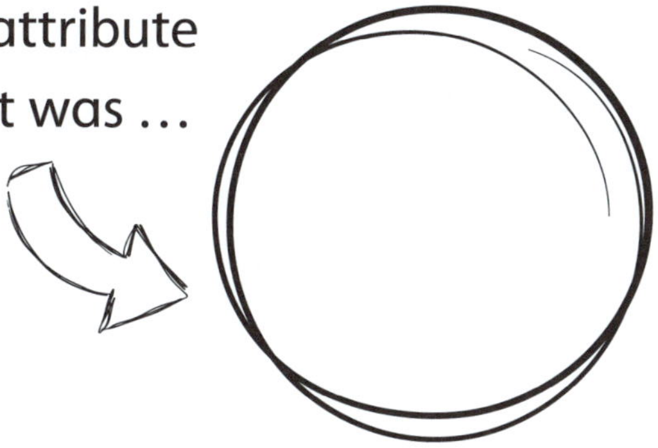

The book I loved the most …

A memory I'll keep …

Next year, I hope to …

# How have I changed this year?

How have you changed this year?

I used to …

Now I can …

 How do you feel when you reflect on your year?